Looki

EASTER BUNNY

A Book of Rhyming for Grades 2-3
BUILDING LITERACY

by

VIOLA GRAYS-WILEY

DEDICATION

This book is dedicated to all the
Early Learners who would
like to master the skill
of rhyming and
have fun while
enjoying a
Great Story!

Looking for the

EASTER BUNNY

A Book of Rhyming for Grades 2-3

BUILDING LITERACY

Can you find all the RHYMING WORDS in this story?

I'm the Easter Bunny.

Buckle up!

This is going to be funny.

I may as well let you know
that everybody is looking
for me.
Last night, I was
hanging out
in a backyard tree.

They were screaming
all over the
neighborhood,
but I'm pretty
sharp, stuff like
that is no good.

I thought

some of the kids

would've figured

this out,

but they were

riding their bikes

going north,

all the while

I was happily
hopping on
my way south.
You see, I'm not a
regular bunny like
my Cousin Bugs,
I got skills for days,
just like
Grandma got hugs.

You might want to

hire a detective

on this case.

No need for the police,

just like you need

fresh air,

that's how I feel

about mace.

Handcuffs won't
hold me,
I can slip them
right off,
before you say
"Good Morning"
Or even cough.

Skills!

Look into my eyes, there's a bunny story.

Look at my feet, there's a lot of glory!

You see, folks been
trying to get a hold
of me since 2019.

They thought they
knew my location,
they found out,
it was just my steam.

Fast Bunny!

I'm one fast bunny,
I've got to say
it myself.

Every time
they turn right,
I know to go left.

You know rabbit
sense is hard to
come by,
but when you got it,
you got it,
and that makes
me so happy,
sometimes, it makes
me cry.

People been looking

for me everywhere,

looked in Jewel Osco,

but I wasn't there!

I know people heard
that I was pink, purple,
white and blue,

But sometimes, folks,

I'm invisible, too.

You see, I can't tell

you my secrets,

that's not what I do.

Don't ask me for ID,

I got one for me,

and one for you.

Rabbit Skills!

So, if you see me driving

in my bunny-mobile,

you keep it moving,

and I certainly will.

'Cause some folks

think I should have

them a basket of eggs,

you see, I ate them

last week

each night before

I went to bed.

I am a respectful

bunny, I say my

prayers and stuff,

but I'm not trying

to go to jail,

some chicken gave

me those eggs,

I told her

that was enough!

I know if I had one

eyewitness, that would

clear this whole thing up,

but it was just me

and the chicken,

who was looking

for a duck.

I told this chicken

I was going to

appear as a suspect,

because folks can't

understand seeing a
rabbit near a
chicken nest.

Out here in Bunny World,
we try to keep
everything on the
down low,

but when you start

talking about jailhouse,

this bunny got to go!

I'm really a laid-back
Bunny from the
other side of town,
I try to follow
the rules and
not act a clown!

The bottom line is
I really don't know
why so many folks
looking for the
Easter Bunny.
I hang around most
of their houses,
whether it's cloudy
or sunny.

I am not a thief.

Those eggs were given

to me, but the next time,

I'm going to make sure

the chicken gives

me

A RECEIPT!

#*thegoodbunny*

#*iminnocent*

THE END

Made in the USA
Las Vegas, NV
21 September 2021